Where, oh Where is Mrs Brown?

A play by Vivian French

Illustrated by Robin Boyden

Characters

Teenager

Dad of twins

Teenager: There's a notice on the door.

Dad: Yes. It says, "Back in five minutes. Mrs Brown".

Jax: Dad! DAD! Let's go!

Mo: Yes, I want to make our cake!

Dad: We can't make the cake without flour, Mo. Just wait – I'm sure Mrs Brown will be back soon.

Teenager: Someone's coming. Maybe it's Mrs Brown.

Grandma Figgs: Now, let me see. Have I got my list, Archie?

Grandpa Figgs: Missed? What have we missed? Have we missed the bus?

Grandma: Not missed, Archie. I said LIST! Oh! Here it is. In my bag …

Jax: Are you the shop lady?

Grandpa: The top lady? What top lady? What's the child saying, Aggie?

Grandma: We've come to buy potatoes. Haven't we, Archie? POTATOES!

Teenager: You'll be lucky. The shop's shut.

Mo: I want to go home – **now**!

Grandma: The note says Mrs Brown will be back in five minutes.

Dad: But we've been here ten minutes already.

Grandpa: Oh dear! I wanted a baked potato for my supper.

Grandma: Well, it's all your fault. You bought the wrong things this morning.

Grandpa: But salt and pepper and flour **always** come in useful, Aggie love.

Grandma: Not when we need potatoes!

Mo: Pssst! Dad!

Dad: What is it, Mo?

Mo: The old man's got flour! **We** need flour!

Grandpa: You like flowers? What a nice child. Did you hear that, Aggie?

Teenager: What do you need flour for, kid?

Jax: It's our birthday, and we're making a great big chocolate cake.

Mo: We've mixed up the sugar and the butter and the eggs –

Jax: But we ran out of flour!

Grandma: What a shame.

Teenager: Hey! I've just had a thought! Have you got any extra butter and eggs?

Dad: Yes. Lots. Why?

Teenager: We can swap! You give me butter and eggs, and I'll give you ... erm. What do you need?

Grandpa: I would **so** like a little baked potato for my supper.

Teenager: **Potatoes**! I've got **loads** of potatoes!

Mo: So you could give **them** some potatoes...

Grandma: And we can give you children a bag of flour.

Mo: And then we can make our cake!

Jax turns to the Teenager.

Jax: And we'll give **you** the butter and eggs.

Teenager: Yes – let's go and get that birthday tea sorted.

Dad: Come on, then!

Grandpa: What? What? What?